To Moira
Best wishes

R C Lemper

Elda E. Lemperey

Avignon to Croxteth

First Published 2004 by Countyvise Limited,
14 Appin Road, Birkenhead, Wirral CH41 9HH

Copyright © 2004 Maureen Lavelle

British Library Cataloguing in Publication Data.
A catalogue record for this book is available from the British Library.

ISBN 1 901231 43 7

Cover Design by Vicki Fogarty inspired by an idea of Raymond's friend Colin Langeveld.

Avignon to Croxteth

The journey of Raymond Lempereur -

chef to a stately home

by
Maureen Lavelle

Raymond Lempereur

Avignon to Croxteth

Raymond Lempereur - chef to Lord Sefton

His first circuit of the spacious Victorian kitchen took in the large wooden tables, the high glass roof letting in plenty of light but quickly losing any heat and the box in the centre of one table. On closer inspection he made an instant decision, gesturing to the kitchen maid he pointed to the bin. She brought it closer, he lifted the nearest bottle, Brown Sauce, it was dropped into the bin. Looking closer at the next bottle he read, Anchovy Sauce, Raymond could not contain his disgust - a chef should make his own sauces, then bottled coffee - sacrilege to a Frenchman. They would all have to go. As the kitchen maid's eyes grew wider he dropped bottle after jar into the bin. 'Cook needed these' she spluttered, but shaking his head Raymond continued until the box was empty. It too went into the now overflowing bin.

Now he could work. Alone in the big kitchen he started his preparations not realising his mistress had entered the kitchen. 'Lempereur', the Countess paused waiting for a reply. 'Lempereur' she repeated. Raymond continued to stir. Her tone altered, 'Chef', he smiled inwardly, at the age of 24 he was now Head Chef to the Earl and Countess of Sefton at their country seat, Croxteth Hall near Liverpool. He intended to be treated with the respect his position commanded.

He turned to his employer. The Countess was standing near the doorway, looking every inch the glamorous model she had been before her marriage. 'Yes My Lady?' he answered. 'Do you have everything you require?' He watched as her green eyes looked from the silver cigarette holder to the table. 'Where is my ashtray?' she turned to the worried maid who had now returned after throwing out the offending bottles and jars. 'I do not have smoking in my kitchen My Lady'. In the silence that followed, Raymond's broken English and authority were being tested. The maid quickly produced the shell shaped ashtray banished by the chef. The Countess knocked the offending ash from the end of the cigarette before leaving. He tried to contain his sigh of relief, his wishes had been accepted, his reign had begun, the Countess never again smoked in his kitchen.

He sent his first meal, Lobster in Aspic, upstairs then waited for the dishes to return. He needed to know if he had tempted his employer's appetite. The salver came down empty, it had all been eaten. Pleased with his efforts he retired for the night.

Lobster in Aspic

After breakfast next morning he was surprised to see the tall figure of Lord Sefton entering the kitchen. 'Good morning Chef'. 'Good morning My Lord' Raymond waited apprehensively to hear the reason for this unexpected visit. 'I must tell you' said the Earl leaning against the heavy wooden kitchen table, 'It's a long time since we had food presented so well at the Hall, keep it up' and after a short chat he left the kitchen. Raymond found it hard to contain his pride and pleasure. He was off to a good start.

It was 1949 - England was picking itself up after the second world war. Raymond, with the help of friends at his previous employment, the residence of the French Ambassador in London, had secured the post of Chef but not without misgivings. He had been working under the direction of a previous chef to the Duke and Duchess of Windsor when he had to make a choice, to work for the film magnate Alexander Korda who needed a chef on his yacht. That had offered a short term position but his prospects seemed better and safer in England, even though the pay of £20 a week with Korda had been tempting. He decided to go north to Croxteth. The previous 24 hours had changed his life for ever.

The journey from the palatial surroundings of the Ambassador's private mansion in Kensington Palace Gardens, London, had taken him from England's capital city through a land trying to recover from the ravages of the second world war. The train had passed bomb sites and rebuilding and deposited him in the port of Liverpool.

Standing on the platform at Liverpool's Lime Street railway station the previous evening he'd waited, his bags by his feet and his hopes high. The station emptied as passengers were met but Raymond stood alone. Time passed slowly and still no-one came to meet him as promised. The large clock was striking seven as the tall policeman who had been watching him adjusted his heavy woollen cape and came towards him. 'What are you waiting for?' he questioned. Raymond remained silent, his first encounter with a northern English accent made even more difficult by the nasal tones familiar to Liverpool.

He tried to explain to an equally confused policeman before reaching into his pocket to produce the 'Croxteth' headed letter. In an instant everything changed, 'Stay there' ordered the officer and walking across the station returned with a taxi. Raymond sank gratefully into the soft leather seat as the policeman gave instructions to the driver. He was driven through the city streets and out into the countryside.

Croxteth in winter snow

Finally the car turned through a large gateway into the Croxteth Park estate, it continued on through fields and parkland. In the distance through the trees he could see the Hall. His eyes widened. Had he made the right decision? It was too late now to question his ability.

The impressive building set in formal grounds, its silhouette outlined against the evening sky oozed tradition and grandeur. As the car swept past the tall pillars fronting the imposing entrance and came to a halt round the back at the servants entrance he took a deep breath. 'That'll be ten bob' (50p) said the driver interrupting Raymond's thoughts, an amount he had not planned to spend. After knocking on the solid wooden door, he turned the huge ring handle to be met by a woman from the kitchen. 'Come in, come in' she said as the taxi driver struggled with his luggage. The Butler arrived 'The Countess has been asking for you' he said, 'Follow me' As they moved along the bare passage a swish of evening gown topped by red hair came towards him 'Good evening' said the Countess, 'Did you have a good journey?' then as an afterthought she added 'Why are you so late arriving?' A shocked Raymond stared into her large green eyes and started to explain about the policeman and the taxi. She seemed surprised. 'I sent the car for you' she stated and swept away . He was to find out much later that the chauffeur had not been told to pick him up! He came to know his mistress as a wonderful lady but, he would find, rather forgetful.

She had married the Earl in 1941. At the time he was one of England's most eligible bachelors and a member of The Prince of Wales set, along with Lord and Lady Mountbatten, Lord and Lady Brownlow and

Josephine - Countess of Sefton

others including her fellow American friend, Wallis Simpson who probably introduced them. It had been the Brownlow's chef who had recommended Raymond for the position at Croxteth.

The Countess was a very considerate employer. One of the first things she did was to collect Raymond from the kitchen and take him in her car for a tour of the estate. Croxteth Park was big, much bigger than he had imagined, but he felt safer than in London. The estate was vast, over 1300 acres. The Hall itself had over 200 rooms and a history that could be traced back almost 900 years through 31 generations to William the Conqueror.

They went to the walled garden where he met the Head Gardener who would provide most of the vegetables for the kitchen. Then to the Farm, meeting the Manager responsible for supplying the kitchen with eggs, dairy produce and some meat. Out into the estate to see the Head Gamekeeper who supervised the rearing of game later to provide sport for the Earl and his guests and eventually to the Head Chauffeur. Their journey then continued into Liverpool to meet the fishmonger and butcher used by the house and finished at Coopers, a magnificent and prestigious store that supplied the household groceries. Here the Countess introduced him to the Manager who was duly informed that Raymond now had her permission to order anything he required, a great responsibility but also a privilege and position of trust.

Living a distance from the Hall, but coming in each day to work were the estate tradesmen, 2 electricians, 2 builders, 3 painters, 2 plumbers, 2 woodmen, a boilerman and a handyman. Gardeners and gamekeepers lived closer as all were employed to help running the estate.

Like most aristocratic families the Seftons carried out an unchanging ritual during the year. The Earl was Chairman of Chester Race Course and Steward at Aintree, Newbury, Newmarket and Royal Ascot, so many of the visitors were connected with horses and racing.

One of the more popular house parties was for Aintree Races; the Earl's ancestors had been involved in the beginnings of the Grand National and owned Aintree Racecourse. Guests staying at the Hall were joined by others who came for the day, finishing off with dinner at the Hall. During the 1960s one of these gatherings was ruined by a robbery at the Hall. On the day of The Grand National race lady guests woke to find their jewels had been stolen along with those of the Countess. She was particularly upset at losing items of great sentimental value including a watch with the numerals marked with diamonds, given to her by The Earl as an engagement present. All the staff, with the exception of the Butler, valet, Lady's maid and Chef were questioned but the missing items were never found. She fared slightly better after a robber took her jewel case on the London to Liverpool train. Some of the items taken then were recovered ten years later.

Riding was a regular event and the Stud an important part of the estate. Hare Coursing, another event started by his ancestors, took place on their land at nearby Altcar during the early spring. Guests came for the pheasant shoots at Croxteth and grouse shoots at their estate of Abbeystead near Lancaster, about 40 miles to the north.

For all these occasions and many more Raymond and his staff of 2, (an assistant to prepare vegetables and a washer-up cleaning woman) catered. His helpers came in from 9.00am until 2.00pm and again in the evening from 6.00 till 9.00 or even 10.00pm, each day. When the house was full and meals were needed for 30 or more people he had one extra helper. His days were long and busy.

He also cooked for the Hall staff - butler, housekeeper, valet, footman, 2 housemaids, and lady's maid, but Raymond always ate alone or with the kitchen staff. Food was plentiful and he was given a free hand to choose and prepare it. There was always meat and vegetables for lunch, usually provided by the estate, followed by a sweet and often fish at night. For the Earl and his guests he would delight in taking extra care and effort not only to cook well but to serve and present his creations with flair.

He never had an interview for the post, and needed no references. The Countess heard of his skills on the grapevine and after speaking to him on the telephone secured his services. At the time he was working for the French Ambassador learning his trade with a chef who had served the Duke and Duchess of Windsor. He couldn't leave the security of his house (considered French territory) without a work permit, but this was soon arranged by Lady Sefton. He arrived at Croxteth in time for the Glorious Twelfth, (beginning the shooting season) and then worked solidly for 14 months before taking a break. His employers then went away so he took the opportunity to return to his homeland in December 1950 and collect his bride. The Countess asking before he left 'You will come back Chef?'

The Seftons were going to America for the holidays and she needed reassuring her chef would be there on her return. A local cook was brought in to feed the staff while they and Raymond were absent. This was to happen occasionally, but when Raymond returned after one trip his 'safely put away' bottle of gin (his relaxant and painkiller for his grumbling appendix) had disappeared. The replacement cook obviously had the same taste as himself. From then on he found a better 'safe place'.

One of his first priorities was to learn English. The Countess spoke fluent French having lived in Paris for the years before her marriage, as did their secretary. The Earl was later to tell Raymond 'Your English can be better than my French' as Raymond conferred with them over his menus while struggling to improve his English. He worked hard to learn the new language. The Earl took 10 daily newspapers and when they had been cleared from the drawing room each night, Raymond would take them to his room to savour. He would sit with his dictionary at his side putting words to pictures and trying to make sense of the text. During his afternoon break (when possible he was off duty between two and four o'clock) he would often visit the cinema in the nearby village of West Derby, where he tried to extend his vocabulary and knowledge of the language.

Sometimes he would go into Liverpool to one of the many cinemas in the city which offered more choice of films, but as he didn't know the bus routes, this often meant a long walk of 5 or 6 miles back to Croxteth Park. At other times he would ride his bike to explore his new home. On one occasion cycling to the nearby coast for some sea air he couldn't find his route back, so had to follow the coastline into Liverpool and then return to Croxteth by road.

Westerns were a particular favourite but not much help with the language used in a stately home. One afternoon they were showing 'Waterloo Bridge' starring Robert Taylor (a favourite) and Vivien Leigh. Raymond had already seen this film in Marakesh - dubbed into French. Knowing the story he could now follow the English soundtrack. Such good luck did not happen often so an enjoyable afternoon supplied an easy lesson that day.

As well as speaking English he had to learn to read and write his new language, but found the hardest part was numbers. England was still counting and measuring in imperial units and money was pounds, shillings and pence - very difficult for a man brought up using decimals. As he kept himself apart from the other staff he didn't have much chance of learning through casual conversation but the chauffeur was a great help to him. Within a year he felt he had command of his new language.

When Raymond returned home to marry Elda in 1950 they had only seen each other for short periods totalling 2 months in two and a half years but many letters allowed them to keep in touch and get to know one another. His employers were away from Croxteth giving him time to take his bride for a short honeymoon.

They went to Marseilles and Paris, visiting the sights and the Folies Bergère before returning to England. As the ship set sail, he had to reassure his very apprehensive 19 year old wife, upset at the thought she might never see her homeland again. Passing through customs they became separated, 'Raymond, Raymond' he heard Elda call; she had no English and no idea where she was going. Her cries of panic brought him back laughing to claim her.

Travelling on the Golden Arrow steam train they journeyed to London and onto The Regency, a 500 roomed hotel, for a few nights. The beautiful bedroom with the green velvet curtains and breakfast served in their room was to leave a

Marriage of Raymond & Elda

lasting impression. The stay cost Raymond 6 guineas per night and gave them the chance to sample 'upstairs' life by putting their shoes outside the door for someone else to clean. Before leaving London they made time to have a meal and chat with his old friend the chef at the Belgian Embassy. Then came the final leg of their journey, a train ride north to Liverpool, finally reaching there on 20th December.

In the taxi Raymond coached Elda in English ready to meet the rest of the staff. By the time they reached Croxteth her 'Good Morning' was word perfect making them think she understood every word they said. It took a lot longer for her to be able to converse with them.

Arriving at their new home they found welcoming flowers had been placed in their quarters behind the kitchen along with a wedding present from the Earl and Countess, a lamp for the new Madame Lempereur. Raymond although pleased was now back in his place of work, 'I have something to show you' he said, and opening a drawer gestured Elda to come and look. Waiting for her attention were 25 pairs of socks needing repair!

As his employers were away they had a month's extension to their 'honeymoon' and with only the staff to cater for they could savour their first Christmas together. Raymond cooked and served an enormous turkey with all the trimmings, but plum pudding and mince pies were unknown dishes to Elda and it would be many years before she enjoyed their strange taste.

The large house was silent with its owners away, so after lunch they wrapped up well against the cold and took out the bikes. As they cycled around the quiet deserted roads the dull grey sky of this new country made Elda depressed. She was used to the French custom of everyone being out and about on Christmas Day. Within weeks Lord and Lady Sefton returned and the house geared up for the Hare Coursing Season culminating with the Waterloo Cup.

This was another of the sporting events closely connected with Croxteth and was held annually at nearby Altcar. The tens of thousands of spectators who made the journey to witness the skill of the greyhounds taking part had, on occasion, outnumbered those who watched the Grand National.

At a dinner held during the Hare Coursing meeting the gold Waterloo Cup stood in the centre of the white damask tablecloth and the place settings were shown off with the Waterloo Chain, made to commemorate the event, draped around the table. An extra gold link was added each year and a small gold plaque with the winner's name engraved. The Earl's dog 'So Clever' was to win in 1971.

Waterloo Cup table setting

The Countess agreed with Raymond's decision not to mix with the rest of the staff. When Elda joined him she too had to keep herself apart but made a friend of the chauffeur's wife who helped with her English. On her arrival at Croxteth Lord Sefton made one of his rare visits to the kitchen, 'Chef' he said with a smile, 'Your wife is very young'. Elda was 19 but looked even younger. Raymond by now knew this meant his master approved and from then on the Earl and Countess always addressed Elda as 'Madame' and the rest of the staff followed suit.

Another time he said to Elda, 'Madame, you have a rival'. 'Have I my Lord?' she asked, thinking there must be a new housemaid. 'Yes' he answered laughing, 'A nice young French filly in my stables'. Praise indeed to be compared to his horses. Raymond worked long hours in the kitchen and Elda had no income of her own so, with the help of the Countess, she got a job at one of the dressmakers used by Lady Sefton in Liverpool.

She had been apprenticed to a dressmaker in France, only giving it up to nurse her mother. To get into the city Elda would leave Croxteth early each day around 7.30 am, cycle to one of the lodges at the edge of the estate and leave her bike there. She could then catch a bus nearby to take her into Liverpool and walk to her job. With Raymond's phrase book in her pocket she could converse with her fellow workers, learning as she went. The return journey was equally long, Elda often getting home at 7.00 pm or later, to find Raymond busy in his kitchen. They did not have much time together and in order to see him she would often join him there and help by preparing vegetables under his direction. He would show her how to cut and prepare them for table presentation.

Elda

During the summer months, the soft fruit season, they were kept very busy 'sorting'. Each day fruit was brought in from the walled garden. The best was used for desserts to be served 'upstairs' or frozen for use during the winter months. The not so firm were served to the staff and the over-ripe and bruised fruit turned into purees and puddings.

After a while Raymond found himself without a kitchen maid - this happened regularly as staff moved on. Elda said 'I'll come and help you, at least we can be together'. Raymond approached the Countess with the suggestion that Elda work with him on a permanent basis. 'Do as you please' she said, 'It's alright with me'. So his wife joined him in the kitchens, and another woman did the cleaning jobs.

Slowly Raymond introduced improvements to the kitchen, the large wooden tables were covered with a washable fabric eliminating the daily 'scrub'. Flooring was laid over the cold and dusty concrete and the old worn out wooden sinks, that gave many a scullery maid splinters in her hands, were replaced with modern stainless steel. But even the new beige painted walls and strip lighting could not make it much warmer. The kitchen stayed true to its designer's plans for keeping food cool. Water left out overnight during the winter months would often have a thick layer of ice on top by morning

Croxteth kitchen and flat entrance

Their flat down the corridor became a warm haven to return to after a busy day. Slowly they added furniture and carpets of their own to personalise it.

From then on they worked as a team, Elda receiving £2 per week for an intended 6 hours work each day. Although her hours became much longer her pay never altered for the next 7 years, but after a meeting with the Estate Manager it went up to £3 per week making her feel suddenly rich.

Now life became easier and more enjoyable as they could organise their off duty time, take their bikes and go out cycling. Covering the prepared tea sandwiches with a damp tea towel gave them longer for outings. On fine days they would cross the River Mersey and spend the afternoon at the resort of New Brighton.

Lord Sefton liked his chef to be available at all times so was not happy when Raymond requested a night off, early in his service, to attend the Bastille Day celebrations. Raymond and Elda were registered with the French Consul in Liverpool. All foreign nationals were required to register with the Embassy of their homeland and in this way kept in touch with other French people living and working locally. Each year he held the celebration on 14th July and each year Raymond would request the night off. Finally he was told, 'Well if you must'. Even though he left the food prepared and ready for serving, the Earl was still not pleased, but a precedent had been set and from then on they attended every year.

His chance for a break would come when the Seftons went to stay at their London home for racing at Goodwood and the Derby. Lady Sefton would say 'We'll be away for a while, you might as well take your time off'. A local cook tended to the Earl and Countess at Sefton House, their London home, where the accommodation was smaller. Only the staff were left to be catered for at Croxteth.

Every 2 years Raymond and his wife returned to see their families in France. This annoyed the rest of the staff who had only one weeks holiday each year. In later years Lord Sefton purchased his own 6 seater plane which upset the staff even more. Now he could return home quicker from his trips away cutting down the staff's break. Raymond heard more than one member of staff utter, 'You've got to be a foreigner to get longer holidays' but he continued to enjoy his employer's generosity.

Although the Seftons often went to America together his Lordship sometimes returned alone, leaving his wife to make her regular visits to her mother. This gave Raymond the chance to serve his Lordship different foods without the Countess altering his menu. On her return these 'new' meals would appear on the menu sent up for her approval each day. She would often bring an American recipe for him to try out, Virginia Cheesecake from her home state, was one that became a favourite along with Virginian style baked Ham.

Virginia ham in Aspic

Routines

Croxteth had a strict and traditional routine, the boilers would be stoked early each morning by the odd job man who would bring the milk for the day from the farm. He would then cycle to the village for the newspapers. He would top up the Aga cooker with coal, returning each evening to keep it going. The only time it was allowed to cool down completely was for its annual clean and service while 'upstairs' were away. Each afternoon he delivered cream, butter and a second delivery of milk to the kitchen, more if guests were due.

Raymond soon fitted into the routine of the house, he would rise by 7.00am and go straight to his kitchen to start on the breakfast. Within a short time he realised precious time could be saved by doing a lot of preparation the previous evening.

Breakfast was served to the staff at 8.00 am in their own dining room, usually egg, bacon, toast; at 8.45 his Lordship was served in the Breakfast Room. There would be a selection of kedgeree or different dishes, rolls and always eggs with bacon, and a tray of cold meats; he always enjoyed a full English breakfast.

At 9.00 her Ladyship would have hers served in her room, usually continental style, rolls or French croissants and coffee, unless she was going out for the day, then she would breakfast earlier in the dining room.

Lunch was at 12.00 noon for the staff and consisted of meat, potatoes, 2 vegetables eg carrots and peas and a sweet, usually fruit or sponge and custard. Upstairs was served at 1.15 in the Dining Room - always a starter and a main course followed by a sweet

If there were guests for shooting, lunch would be packed into the hot boxes and sent out. Usually there was a beef stew or steak and kidney pudding made with port and brandy, sometimes individual chicken pies served with plenty of vegetables followed by a hot ginger or honey pudding with cream, occasionally a cold sweet. There would always be plenty of fresh bread rolls and small pots of hot coffee.

A table would be set out in one of the huts or at a nearby farm and the food served in silver dishes just as if the guests were at the Hall, the only thing missing being the candelabra. On one occasion the jugs of coffee went out with only hot water, luckily a member of staff who had gone to wait on managed to quickly send for the missing coffee and none of the guests realised.

Afternoon tea was taken upstairs in the Sitting Room at 5.00 pm, always two lots of sandwiches, one of which was usually cucumber and a selection of cakes, maybe crumpets in cold weather.

The staff took their evening meal at 6.00 pm often a fish or meat dish.

Dinner for upstairs was at 8.00pm- 8.30 if the Earl and Countess had been out racing or shooting. This would be five or six courses, soup, then fish, the main course of meat with a selection of vegetables and potatoes, a sweet and the cheese board with coffee. They would always dress for dinner, even when there were only the two of them the Countess wore an evening gown and her jewellery and the Earl a dinner suit, always of velvet - standards never slipped!

Although Raymond created wonderful dishes for 'upstairs' their own 'tasting' sessions were confined to any uneaten food returning to the kitchen in the silver dishes. This was often the case with food that couldn't be kept or used up in another dish. Gifts for the Countess, like her favourite caviar were sampled (but only once as neither of them enjoyed the taste!). One night he served a particular favourite of his mistress, Vacherin, a creation of pears and cream in 3 layers of meringue, only a small portion was eaten so Raymond and Elda enjoyed the rest.

Next day a note was sent to the kitchen 'Could we please have the rest of the Vacherin'. Raymond rushed to create a replacement, cutting out the 'eaten' portion before sending it upstairs. After lunch the Countess visited her chef, 'That was not the same one was it?' she asked. 'Oh certainly My Lady' replied Raymond - her face showed she was not convinced. Lord Sefton would use the phrase 'It's been USED' to show staff he knew what had happened.

During the season the first day's shoot was always rushed back to the Hall to be cooked for dinner that evening. The kitchen staff would pluck the pheasants or grouse for Raymond to cook. Extra birds would be 'sent out' for plucking. A local girl was paid 6d (2½p) per bird and would often do as many as 60 at a time. The chicks were reared on the estate by gamekeepers who fed them a diet including sultanas and currants to sweeten their meat. Whatever was 'bagged' on following days went into the freezer.

Grouse

When the guests were at nearby Altcar for shooting pheasant or partridge the gunloaders and chauffeurs also had to be fed making it a very long and full day for Raymond and his helper. His priorities were always to have meals cooked for upstairs first, then staff, followed by the loaders and finally the kitchen. His own meals were taken late when he first arrived but as he organised the kitchen he found an earlier slot for himself and Elda to eat.

On starting at Croxteth Raymond was informed His Lordship did not eat garlic and was not fond of onions, neither were to be used in the Earl's food. How was a French chef to cook without one of his staple flavouring ingredients? He sifted, grated, liquidised, strained and used any other method he could think of. The Earl had garlic regularly for the next 24 years without realising it. When Raymond sent minestrone soup sprinkled with garlic and parsley the Butler told him, 'That'll be sent back, I can smell garlic, you know what the Earl is'. The plates returned empty . Raymond congratulated himself.

Earl of Sefton

The Earl enjoyed good food and he provided it. Over the years he put on weight and Lady Sefton would tease him and try to put him on a diet. To please her he would miss either the fish or soup course and maybe a sweet, to try to lose a few pounds. In the end she just arranged for his trousers to be let out!

The Countess had different taste, she loved his onion soup and whenever the Earl was away it was always served to her. She very much enjoyed pasta, an uncommon taste in England in the 1950s and asked 'Chef, can you make fresh pasta?'. 'Of course' he said, 'I'm an expert at that', then delegated the job to Elda. Her noodles coloured green with pureed spinach were a particular favourite. The first time she used spinach to colour the pasta it was cooked, drained, put through a mincer then a sieve and finished off by wringing it through a muslin cloth held at each end by Raymond and a kitchen maid. Unfortunately they twisted too hard and the cloth burst sending spinach juices flying around the kitchen. The resulting sight of a chef, kitchen maid, pans and assorted surfaces running with green would have astonished 'upstairs' but the note that came down later said it was 'superb' which thrilled Elda. From then on they mixed the 'spinach pulp' with flour and eggs to produce green pasta, particularly tagliatelle to serve with a Napolitan sauce, a favourite starter for the Countess - this also meant the entire kitchen didn't need cleaning every time it was served.

Another of her favourites was curry but it took Raymond a while to get to know her taste. The first time he served it to her she announced it was 'alright-but could be hotter'. Next time he doubled the amount of spices expecting a good result but back came her verdict, 'better - but still not hot enough' After a few weeks it was on the menu again. Raymond put ALL his spices into the dish. The curry was so hot he perspired himself when he later tasted it. Back came the comment, 'beautiful!' It was third time lucky for Raymond who had decided the Countess' taste buds were as fiery as her red hair.

The Hall had a regular turnover of staff, particularly housemaids. They would come from Ireland and Italy as well as England. Often using the job as a reason for coming into England. Footmen seemed to stay longer and often started younger. Part of the duties of one young man was to light the staff fire before the rest of the staff came down. He regularly slept late and would rush downstairs then set light to paper in the fireplace then return upstairs to finish dressing. The rest of the staff on seeing smoke coming from the chimney would presume the fire lit and venture downstairs into a very cold staff area. He was eventually lured away by the promises of a better job by a house guest.

Another footman became a bit cheeky, a habit Raymond felt lacked the respect he deserved. One day he came to collect the staff's lunch and hovered eagerly over the pancakes Raymond was preparing. 'Would you like one?' Raymond asked. 'Please' replied the hungry footman eating it quickly. 'Want another?' 'Yes please' 'Take up the tray and then come back' said Raymond. On his return he grabbed the waiting pancake stuffing his mouth, his eyes streamed and he clutched at his throat as he realised Raymond had taken his revenge. It had been full of strong French mustard. Unable to speak he fled the kitchen to gulp glasses of water in the staff pantry. His red face and streaming eyes were still in evidence when he entered the staff dining room. 'You've been annoying the chef again haven't you!' they choroused. At least he fared slightly better than the small footman who became such a nuisance Raymond bundled him into the dumb waiter (food lift) and left him there to stew a while!

During Raymond's time as chef the house had 4 or 5 housekeepers, one of the most prestigious positions in the Hall. One came from London. He answered a knock at his kitchen door to see a tall, slim lady who said 'Can you bring my luggage in?' as she walked past him. 'Who are you?' he asked not used to being spoken to like her servant. 'Wait here while I get the Butler', but meeting a footman he handed her over and returned to his kitchen. She told everyone she had worked for Queen Mary and kept to herself taking all her meals in her room, but her ideas were very different from those of the staff at Croxteth and her stay was short.

Visitors

Croxteth Hall

During his 24 years at Croxteth he cooked for many visitors. Most of the time he was given ample warning of who was coming and what was needed, but not always. During his first winter there in November 1949 Lady Sefton arrived in the kitchen at about 10.00 o'clock at night. 'Chef' she said, 'I meant to tell you, The Queen (Queen Mum) is attending the races so she will be taking tea here with the 2 princesses tomorrow afternoon. Can we have a large gateau?' 'It's a bit late' Raymond said almost to himself. 'What will we do?' she implored. 'We' was to become one of the phrases Raymond got to know as the Countess 'forgot' to mention many visitors.

His mistress returned to the kitchen early next day. 'Chef?' she enquired looking around. He sent the maid to the pantry with the instruction to bring her Ladyship whatever was there. She returned with a large gateau, the surprised Countess asking 'Where did that come from?' was told 'I was up at 3.00 am to make it', he replied 'I have no other time'. The sigh of relief from his mistress could be heard outside the kitchen.

Among the visitors was Lady Adare, cousin of the Earl. She came from her estate in Ireland. The Seftons 'loaned' Raymond to her before his marriage, while they were visiting America, as she was without her own chef. He flew from Liverpool to Shannon Airport and waited to be met. Over the loudspeaker system came an announcement, 'Would Ms Lempereur go to meet the chauffeur at the gate' Raymond took himself and his bags towards the exit, there waiting for him was a cadillac, one of a fleet owned by the family. He was driven to Limerick and stayed with her in Ireland for 5 weeks. This arrangement helped his finances as he still got paid if his employers were out of the country but Lady Adare also paid him for the time he was with her. Double wages!

Raymond got on well with her and her family, including the children who came to the kitchen to visit and chat, a new experience for Raymond as there were no children at Croxteth.

His first visit to their kitchen was to leave a lasting impression. A large box of 'earth' was positioned next to the cooker. 'What's this?' he asked one of the 3 kitchen maids. 'It should not be in my kitchen'. 'It's your coal' she replied lifting the plate on the hob to show Raymond peat burning well to provide his heat.

He enjoyed cooking for the family but was injured by their storage arrangements. Meat was delivered to him in the kitchen, after inspecting it he would take it to the 'cold room' outside the main house where it was hung till required. Standing on his toes to lift the heavy meat onto a hook it went through his hand, unable to free himself he called for help until someone heard and came to lift him up and release his hand. His priority then was to clean up the 'bloody mess' his hand had made.

Lady Adare and her family all spoke French so there was no difficulty communicating their needs but he was informed his accent 'would not be understood by the suppliers'. So he gave a list of his needs and she would telephone the orders every couple of days. He found their meals different to Croxteth, particularly their regular Sunday habit of eating freshly made ice-

26

cream. The staff were easy to get on with, not as formal as in England. After meals the furniture was often pushed to the sides of the room as someone produced an accordian to play for the impromptu dance.

Running out of toothpaste one day the chauffeur took him to the nearest shop, a long low cottage with small windows that housed the Post Office. The strange smell as he entered was caused by the sheep kept at the other end of the building. Some things he never got used to.

His employers could be equally informal when on a trip to Killarney Lord Adare lent him a hat and coat to accompany the family on a walk beside the Atlantic Ocean. He was almost part of the family watching the passing ships head for America.

On a day out in Limerick Raymond and the chauffeur were admiring leather travel bags in a shop, he decided to buy one. As he was about to pay Lady Adare came up behind him, 'Put that on my bill' she said to the assistant and left the shop. Although Raymond was delighted with her generosity he later wished he'd picked a bigger and better bag!

Before his return to England Lady Adare took him to visit a pair of semi-detached bungalows near the house, one was for her estate manager, and the other she offered to Raymond if he would stay and work for her. She showed him around the eight - roomed house which was luxury compared to his quarters behind the kitchens at Croxteth. Opening the cupboards she pointed to the linen awaiting the new occupant. 'All for you and your wife' she said. 'If you'll stay' 'I'm sorry' said Raymond 'I must return to Croxteth'. His return journey saw him driven by her chauffeur to Limerick to catch a train to Dublin, then the ferry for Liverpool travelling first class courtesy of her Ladyship. She was still hoping to persuade him to return. He took all his meals in his cabin, being first class this meant they were served from silver dishes giving him a small taste of the 'upstairs' life style.

He carried a large parcel for his employers which was examined and opened as he left the ship. It contained a piece of raw Irish beef and he was breaking the law. When questioned he explained who he was and where he was delivering the beef. 'Take it' he was ordered but soon after reaching Croxteth he was summoned to the Secretary's office to find Customs and Excise men waiting to check his story.

On her next trip to England Lady Adare was bold enough to say in Lady Sefton's hearing, 'You've been here too long chef'. Although tempted to work for Lady Adare living in Ireland would have put the Irish Sea as well as the Channel between him and his beloved France. From Liverpool he could reach a Chanel ferry within 5 or 6 hours. The journey from Ireland would be much longer, an easy decision.

Another visitor was an American who so enjoyed Raymond's starter of salmon mousse that he sent to the kitchen for the recipe. Raymond, like most chefs, did not give away his secrets and ignored the request. He was asked again but felt any chef worthy of the name would be able to produce a salmon mousse and did not reply. The next request stated the recipe would be used at the White House and ordered that it be written down. Raymond provided the recipe but left out one of his own ingredients.

Many friends from Hollywood came to stay with the Countess including film stars Errol Flynn and Ray Milland. The maids were most impressed but Elda did not see him. She said to the Countess 'Please could I ask a favour?' 'Yes' was the answer. 'Everyone has seen Ray Milland but me, can you steer him this way?' The Countess was true to her word and later was heard to call from outside the kitchen, 'Madame, Mr Ray Milland is here for you' A very embarassed but thrilled Elda was then asked 'How do you live with this English weather?' as he signed an autograph before pulling his collar up, his trilby further down over his head and going out.

Ray Milland

If Raymond could not be in attendance no-one was permitted to enter the kitchen in case they spoilt (or in the case of staff 'borrowed') anything from his kitchen. This had been noticed by 'upstairs' as Lady Sefton was heard telling her dinner guests one evening, 'I must have the only house in England with a locked kitchen' 'Oh no' said another titled guest, 'My chef locks his kitchen too'.

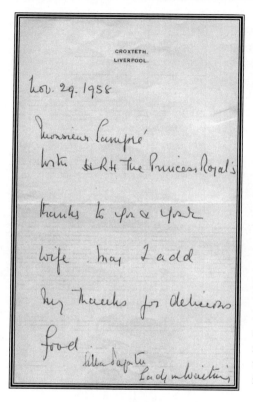

CROXTETH,
LIVERPOOL.

Nov. 29. 1958

Monsieur Lampré
both to HRH The Princess Royal's
thanks to you & your
wife. May I add
my thanks for delicious
food.
Hilda Lapôtre
Lady in Waiting

Note from The Princess Royal

Croxteth Hall often entertained Royalty who had to be particularly well looked after. When the Princess Royal stayed in 1958 Elda was given precise instructions on how to prepare her boiled egg for breakfast. It had to be timed exactly; this she did. After preparing her tray she was informed the Princess was not ready for breakfast, the egg was put to one side and another cooked, the Princess was still not ready and a third egg was boiled. She was later told by her Lady's maid 'the first one would have done'. Before the Princess left, a handwritten note on Croxteth headed notepaper was delivered to the kitchen. It read 'Thanks for the delicious food'.

Accidents rarely happened but making dinner for the Earl and his guests one evening Raymond cut his finger quite badly, he could not stop the bleeding and had to stop cooking. It needed a trip to hospital for stitching but he knew the Earl and his guests, a party of 9, were waiting for their meal. Calling the Butler in to the kitchen he asked 'Can dinner be put back half an hour?' A shocked Butler said 'No'. 'I need treatment' replied Raymond showing his injury. 'It's not possible' continued the Butler without any emotion, 'The Earl is expecting dinner'. Using his own methods Raymond covered his cut finger with the membrane of an onion and then bandages to stem the flow of blood. The Earl was informed of a 'slight delay' before the starter Bosche (beetroot soup) was served and he was heard to joke with his guests that the soup was made with 'chef's blood'.

The same rules applied if Raymond fell ill. Fortunately this did not happen often but he did suffer with severe migraines. He would work in his kitchen as long as possible only retiring to bed when it was impossible for him to carry on. Then Elda would finish. At Croxteth this meant running between the kitchen and their rooms behind to get instructions. At Abbeystead it was a lot more difficult as their bedroom was two floors above the kitchen via many stairs.

One time Raymond was suffering severe stomach pain which he was treating with his usual painkiller, small tots of gin. The pain would not go away and he awoke next morning in agony unable to stand. Crawling from his bed he pulled himself upright and made his way to the kitchen. After supervising breakfast he got out his bike and cycled, in agony, to the nearest Doctors, about 2 miles away. He was diagnosed with appendicitis and ordered to hospital but Raymond's priority was, as always, his kitchen. He returned to Croxteth and going to the office to explain his absence requested a car to take him to hospital. 'The car is not for carting around staff,' said a member of the office staff. The Earl's secretary realising how ill he was took him to hospital arriving at noon and he was on the operating table by 3.00 pm with no time to spare. After a 10 day stay he arrived back at Croxteth and ignoring instructions to convalesce, went straight to the kitchen, as he knew guests were due to attend the Chester Races.

Most staff worked through illness in this way, and although the instructions from 'upstairs' were always 'Just do what you can' the reputation of the house was fiercely guarded and no-one liked to let down their colleagues. When the housekeeper broke her leg she hobbled around with her leg in plaster supervising the other staff.

If time had to be taken off staff would return as soon as possible often before properly recovered. When Raymond had an operation on cartilage in his nose he was told not to go into the kitchen for 2 weeks but after being asked 'When will you be able to start work?' one week later he started cooking, even though the smells caused him pain. He was also advised not to drink for 2 years and feeling fine tried a whisky after just a few months, the vapours hurt the lining of his nose so much he obeyed that instruction for a while longer.

The Earl's regular dinner parties required a lot of work but gave Raymond a chance to be more creative and adventurous with his dishes. Lunch was always 3 courses and Dinner, 5 courses, often for 30 or more people including staff.

The meal was always served by candlelight in the family's silver serving dishes, and staff would be instructed not to touch the silver dishes when serving as the fingerprints would show up in the candlelight.

Silver serving dish

The menu would be displayed on cards edged in gold (costing one shilling (5p) each) written by Elda in gothic script. Guests would each have an individual silver cruet. The table settings were always of the finest china and glass. Dinner parties would often go on late into the night followed by games of bridge until the early hours. Then they would be up just after 7.00am ready for breakfast before going out to shoot.

The Hall was always busy from August through to spring then quieter during the summer months. They could comfortably accommodate 18 guests with their servants for house parties so the staff were kept busy. The Butler would have a list of names and breakfast times for the kitchen. Gentlemen breakfasted in the dining room but Ladies traditionally had theirs on a tray in their rooms. This was usually coffee with scones or toast and a selection of jams and marmalades.

Downstairs the jugs would be filled with hot water to keep them warm until needed then they would be filled with coffee and hot milk to go upstairs. During one shoot a particularly keen footman picked up 2 jugs and placing them on the prepared tray took it up to his mistress only to return shamefaced a short time later. The jugs still contained only hot water as Elda was still preparing the milk.

Racing, shooting or hare coursing visitors made a lot more work for Raymond. Everything was freshly made and seasonal, and only the best quality produce was used. Many of the vegetables were home grown in the large walled garden, beef and pork came from the Home Farm. Groceries, fish and any other meat came from selected suppliers in Liverpool. Lobster and fresh salmon were sent from Aberdeen.

When the Countess forgot to tell chef of visitors, he would sometimes find out via the Butler. On one occasion she invited the entire company of a Liverpool theatre, some 60 people and still said at his shocked face when he found out, 'What are we going to do' but Raymond loved the challenge of catering for all these visitors no matter how much work was needed, he took great pride in always being prepared.

During 1950 a garden party was held with hundreds of people attending. It took the kitchen over 2 days to prepare all the dishes to be served. On the Sunday evening after it was all over Lord and Lady Sefton went away for the week, so the staff also took a well deserved rest.

Another regular guest was Sir Malcolm Sargeant, the conductor. When performing in the area he would stay at the Hall. Lady Sefton brought him down to the kitchens to meet Chef telling him of their new arrival. 'They've got a baby' he beamed, 'How exciting' and strode through the long kitchen demanding to see it. Elda duly pulled the pram into the kitchen from the corridor, 'Beautiful' he praised when he saw their son Michel, and signed an autograph for his growing collection.

Elda had wanted their child to be born in France but could not make the journey alone. Raymond's priority was 'upstairs', so he could not go with her. Elda stayed, their son was born in England and they promised their families they would return to France to have him baptised. By now the bikes had been put to one side and they had invested in a motorbike and side-car. Loading it up with luggage and baby they set off for France after lunch one summer day.

The small family drove through country lanes and past towns and villages (there were no motorways to speed their trip). The first night they stopped at Little

Brickhill near Dunstable. Next morning they continued their journey by catching the ferry across the channel then drove through France. It was more than 1000 miles from Croxteth to Avignon in the south of France and their journey took three and half days. Later they would fly in a matter of hours.

It was not long after this that a permanent return to France was discussed. Raymond and Elda wanted their son to be brought up there and an opening in his uncle's business was imminent. Raymond told the Countess 'In a years time we will be leaving'. She was not pleased, 'We don't want to lose you' she said. They continued with plans for their departure over the coming months, then the uncle changed his mind. When a disappointed Raymond informed the Countess 'I'm staying' she said 'Oh that's marvellous, I'll go and tell Lord Sefton'. Considering a move to the south of England they again changed their minds and stayed, so their son grew more

Lempereur family on Croxteth terrace

English than French and in later years married Annette, the daughter of a man who in his youth had been one of the beaters at Lord Sefton's Shoot, before going on to become a chief engineer for Tate & Lyle.

Visitors to Croxteth

Her Majesty The Queen for tea at Race meeting of November 1950

HRH The Princess Royal   HRH Princess Alexandra

Duke of Norfolk   Duke & Duchess of Gloucester

Duke of Roxburgh   Duke & Duchess of Devonshire

Duke of Roseberry   Lord & Lady Rothschild & family

Earl & Countess of Derby - Stanley family

Lord Leverhulme   Lord and Lady Rocksavage

Lord Caernarvon   Lord Halifax

Lord & Lady Adare *(from Ireland)*   Lady Blandford *(Tina Onassis)*

Lady Beatty   Count & Countess from Mexico

Sir Richard Molyneux *(Lord Sefton's uncle)*

Sir Harcourt Brown   Sir Robert Boothby

Sir Malcolm Sargeant   Lord Rank

Colonel Stirling *(from Scotland)*   American Ambassador

Mr Best *(from America)*   Mr & Mrs Berger *(from America)*

Ms & Mme Verne *(from France)*   Mr Joel *(from S Africa)*

Mr & Mrs Douglas Fairbanks Jnr   Mr & Mrs Ray Milland

Mr Errol Flynn & son   Mr Rex Harrison & Lili Palmer

Countess of Leichtenstein   Sophie Tucker *(singer)*

Lord & Lady Brownlow

and many others

Apple Charlotte

Braised Lettuce and Tomatoes

Chicken in Jelly

Filets de Sole

Filets de Sole Urbain-Dubois

Butter a 'crown' mould, line it diagonally with 12 sole fillets, flattened and seasoned, overlapping with both ends over the rim. Fill the empty space with a fish sauce and mussels, bring back the sole fillets to cover and close the mould, press it down well.

Cook in a bain-marie in a moderate heat. Leave to set before removing from the mould.

Poach scallops then roll in breadcrumbs and fry.

Place 'set' sole fillets in a round dish, cover with Sauce Normande and truffles, garnish the centre hole with prepared scallops.

Serves 4-6 people

Cold Salmon en Bellevue with varied salads

Pear Vacherin

Glazed Topside of Beef

Lobster in Aspic

Moussaka a la Turque (Turkish Moussaka)

Take 3 whole aubergines cut in half lengthways, score and salt the flesh and leave to sweat. Dry on a towel and lightly flour then fry in oil until tender, cool and remove the flesh putting the skins to one side.

Chop well cooked lamb and add an equal amount of chopped aubergine flesh. Add tomato purée, chopped garlic, herbs and one teaspoon of paprika.

Fry tomatoes cut into quarters then add to the meat mixture, remove it from the heat and thicken with 2-3 eggs.

Grease a mould, line it with aubergine skins, pour in the mixture and cook for 40 minutes in a bain-marie in the oven. Allow to cool for 10 minutes then turn out onto a round dish and serve very hot with a spicy tomato sauce.

Chicken Vol au Vent

Moussaka

Lobster in Aspic

Paté de foie en aspic avec truffles

Soles a la Suchet

Remove the skin, open the sole in the middle, remove the fish
bone in the centre. In the opening place half a teaspoon
butter/salt. Place the sole in a buttered dish (open side face
down) and poach slowly with a lid on, in 3 teaspoons of fish
stock with white wine and seasoning.

Drain the fish, place in a dish to keep warm, prepare the sauce.

Sauce Normande (White wine sauce)
Make a roux with butter and flour, add fish stock, wine, salt and
pepper. Add 3-4 egg yolks and cook gently without boiling

Cook carrots, cut in a thin julienne, in butter in a pan with a lid.
While they are cooking prepare a long dish decorating the edges
with pomme duchesse. Dress the cooked sole, cover with the
sauce and garnish with julienne carrots and thinly cut truffle -
serve immediately.

Soles a la Suchet

Spinach with Puff Pastry

Abbeystead

Abbeystead House

The Earl's shooting parties also took place on the grouse moors of his estate of over 18000 acres at Abbeystead near Lancaster (later owned by the Duke of Westminster). The Sefton Family had aquired Abbeystead in the Trough of Bowland during the late 1800s, where they built a smaller version of Croxteth Hall. The beautiful building of grey stone with large windows and sweeping gardens was known as Abbeystead House.

Raymond replaced a resident cook who, according to staff, had consistently upset the Countess. She often ignored the wishes of her mistress when setting menus. Knowing of the Earl's dislike for blueberry pie she would serve it. The maids delighted in telling him of the last time it had been served when the Earl had thrown it out of the window. The cook left the same day.

Abbeystead was presided over by an elderly housekeeper who had served Lord Sefton as a child, by now she was forgetful and inefficient.

The staff quarters were particularly cold and damp, left unattended between one visit and the next. The rooms were not warmed nor the beds aired. In later years staff would blame this for their rheumatics. The uncomfortable conditions continued for the kitchen staff whose meals were served on a bare wooden table. 'Why no tablecloth?' Raymond asked a kitchenmaid. 'You need to see the Housekeeper' he was told. This he did but it was obvious she did not like anyone questioning her authority. When she came to the kitchen later and threw a cloth onto the table an annoyed Raymond followed her and threw the cloth back on her table stating, 'No-one does that to me. I am the chef'. Although she returned later and the table was always properly laid he was soon to realise he had got off to a bad start with an important member of staff.

On his first night the Butler showed him to his sleeping quarters, a room with five beds for footmen and valets. 'Take any bed' he was told. 'I want my own room' he said not pleased with this arrangement. 'Housekeeper's orders' the Butler informed him. Raymond had made an enemy of the elderly woman who resented the young chef. He made a formal request for quarters that befitted his status and soon had his own room.

When he was later joined by his wife and baby he again asked for changes, he wanted a fire in their room. By then it was realised the housekeeper, now over eighty years old, would have to be retired to the comfort of an old people's home. A younger housekeeper brought in a new regime treating the staff with consideration and making sure their quarters were warm and comfortable.

Life had changed little at Abbeystead over the years and the regular trips were a feat of organisation. Everything to cater for the Earl and his guests had to be packed into a lorry and taken from Croxteth by the staff. Raymond took large hampers of food, enough for visitors and staff. Herbs and spices for his recipes, his pots, pans, dishes and most importantly, his knives. Later on it would also carry his baby son's cot and pram.

Raymond and Elda would be driven by the chauffeur in the Earl's limousine with the Butler and her Ladyship's maid. The footmen, valet and other staff would go in the shooting brake and the Earl and Countess would travel in their Rolls Royce. Croxteth Hall was left deserted except for outside staff.

After taking the staff, then his master, the chauffeur would proceed to Manchester airport to pick up the guests. Over time this became a well executed operation. Abbeystead could take about a dozen guests but with gamekeepers and loaders to be fed lunch would be needed for 30 or more staff.

Staff accommodation was as rigid here as in the Victorian days when it was built. Male staff had bedrooms on one floor, female staff on another along with Raymond and his wife. They had very little 'off duty' time often cooking for 35 people each day depending on how many guests had been invited to shoot grouse. Many of them brought a chauffeur, all the gentlemen brought a valet and their wives, a lady's maid.

Kitchen at Abbeystead

The kitchens were old fashioned, even more than Croxteth. The sink was low but the windows were large and low giving colourful views of azaleas and other flowering shrubs. They could also see the activities of the guests out of doors as it overlooked the Gun Room. The house was cold, the corridors never warmed up so a visit to the distant toilets was put off as long as possible. Getting food from the kitchen to the Dining room without it getting cold meant the footman and his trays had to move quickly.

In the Still Room, the housekeeper would prepare the breakfast trays to go to the Ladies bedrooms in the traditional manner, leaving the dining room free for the gentlemen to take a cooked breakfast, prepared by Raymond, before a shoot.

The smaller conditions at Abbeystead often frustrated Raymond, he had a small Aga and an electric cooker with a temperamental thermostat. High, medium and low were the best that could be achieved making cooking difficult and he preferred the Aga. At first he questioned why all his equipment had to be carried back and forth each visit and was told, 'We don't go that often'. A phrase Raymond found hard to understand so he started to build up the kitchen by leaving some pans, dishes and utensils each visit. Then he would replace the equipment at Croxteth with new utensils.

He prided himself on never forgetting anything but on one occasion left behind the parmesan cheese. Although the village had only one shop, the Post Office and one bus a day to Lancaster he was not unduly worried. He could serve a menu without it, that was until the Countess requested it and he had to admit defeat.

Only once was a mistake made over a meal. About ten minutes before dinner the Butler came to collect the menu cards for the dining table. Elda had almost completed writing them, just needing the sweet to be added.

'Souffle au Fromage' said Raymond, (cheese souffle). Elda thought he'd said 'Souffle a L'Orange' (orange souffle) an easy mistake in a busy kitchen. The Butler set out icing sugar and cream, not the thing to add to a cheese souffle! Later in the kitchen an amazed Butler told Raymond of the mistake. He waited for the expected visit by the Countess. She duly arrived, 'What happened Chef?'

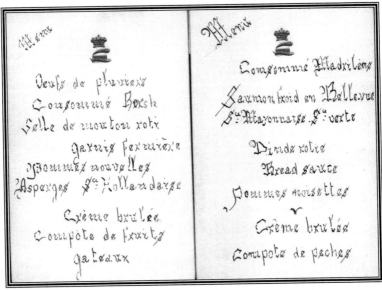

Menu cards

she asked. As he apologised for the mix up he was glad to see her sense of humour when she laughed 'We all had to smell our plates to check what we were eating'. It was his only mistake in 24 years.

Visitors often tipped the staff, particularly the Butler who never shared with other staff. For the older members of staff this was a new perk. They hadn't been allowed to accept money when the old Earl was alive. None ever reached Raymond unless it was in an envelope with his name on until a wealthy businessman came to stay. When he was about to leave he came down to the kitchens to personally thank him for his meals. Shaking his hand Raymond felt the crumpled piece of paper. When the gentleman had gone he unfolded it and swiftly moved out of the kitchen and went to see Elda, 'Look' he said showing her the twenty pound note he had been tipped. A lot of money in 1950 when he was earning £8 a week. There were many 'perks' to be had working in a stately home. Food and board were provided, soaps and toiletries were on hand and they received holiday pay. With these benefits their joint income came to considerably more than the outside staff who earned an average £5 per week each. Later on they were able to afford to fly to France allowing them more time for their holiday.

Abbeystead was beautiful, the Earl affectionately referring to it as the 'shooting lodge'. Raymond and Elda enjoyed the English spring but found the winters so cold! The worst part of living in England was the lack of sunshine. Although missing the warm sun of France they came to love the green moors around and the beauties of the English seasons particularly spring. Daffodils and carpets of bluebells provided a picturesque setting for their regular walks and the subjects for Raymond's growing hobby of photography. Finding it hard to get into town to have his films developed he started his own dark room, developing his pictures alongside his drying teatowels, eventually building an enlarger to help him with his growing collection.

Life was less formal than at Croxteth, 'upstairs' would relax a little. The grown-ups often played childish games like Hide'n'seek while drinking cocktails before dinner, a game the staff found particularly amusing as the Earl and his friends were all over six foot in height. Moving around the smaller house guests and staff came into more contact with each other. The day Raymond was leaving the Butlers pantry and bumped into a beautiful Tina Onassis dressed all in black, stayed in the young man's mind for a long time.

One time at Abbeystead Raymond and Elda were out walking during their off duty time. They met the Earl and Countess out with their guests including Lord and Lady Derby, Lord and Lady Rosebury, and Lord and Lady Devonshire. They paused and introduced them as 'My chef and his wife' then carried on leaving a bemused chef to continue his walk.

Abbeystead gardens

By the 1950s the family were still visiting on a regular basis. Between August and March they would spend at least one week each month at Abbeystead starting with 3 weeks during August. They went for the shooting season but often just for a weekend break. Princess Alexandra continued a tradition of royal visitors and came to Abbeystead when she opened the University of Lancaster. Many guests were to enjoy the hospitality here. At one time they held the record for the number of grouse 'bagged' in a day.

Fishing was also enjoyed by the guests and trout caught at six o'clock in the morning would be sent straight to the kitchen for Raymond to prepare and serve for breakfast.

Early Life/War Years

Avignon

Raymond was born in May 1925 in Avignon. His mother ran the laundry until she died of cancer when he was 4. From then on he was brought up, along with his brother and sister, by their aunt who had her own child and their grandmother, the only person left to show the small child any affection. When they later moved to a villa outside the town they were joined by an uncle. Life was hard and money was short. Meals were often a mix of coffe and milk with bread. His shoes would be stuffed with cardboard to cover the holes so it helped that grandmother was given coupons to help feed and clothe the youngsters.

As a young man he contracted polio - a fact that was to save him in his later years. Because of this he spent many periods in a sanatorium, not seeing friends or family for long stretches of time. His nurse became his focus in life. Attending school between these visits he never noticed the young girl a few years his junior who would one day become his wife.

In 1939, at the age of 14 he needed a job. A position was found for him in a confectionery, (even though he wanted to be a mechanic and advised by the medical profession to get a 'seated' job). He was now on his feet all day and every day but in a career that meant his family would never again go hungry. That same year the world went to war. He continued to learn his profession as life changed around him. He grew to enjoy cooking food and creating dishes.

When the Hotel Terminus needed an apprentice he moved there learning vegetable preparation and ways of cooking meat. He learned a lot from the Commis Chef and as a 16 year old would often return during his off duty hours to watch and develop the skills of boning meat. The canapés and hors d'oevres he saw created would be served at Croxteth in later years.

As he moved between his home and the Hotel he would see the young men trying to obstruct the Germans by slashing their tyres or putting sand in the fuel tanks of their vehicles.

German Officers had requisitioned part of the hotel also dividing the kitchen so their own cooks

Young Raymond aged 19

prepared their food. They were tolerated by the kitchen staff but when they left the kitchen for a break without taking a handgun with them Raymond could not resist a closer look. Taking it from the holster his thoughts started to race but he had to quickly replace it as the cook returned. He looked at the gun swaying slightly in the holster then at Raymond, never again did he leave the kitchen without it.

Food was severely rationed, particularly meat which was only served to German officers. Large pans of sauerkraut with sausage and pieces of pork would cook gently all afternoon so whenever the cooks took a break Raymond and his friend would quickly help themselves from the pot.

It was around this time his brother was lost at sea while returning home on leave from the air force, but Raymond did not have the luxury of time to grieve. He was trying to keep one step ahead of the militia who were sending all healthy young men to work for the Germans. Raymond did not intend to go or to be caught avoiding the 'call up'. These offenders were sent to concentration camps or shot as an example to others.

One day he received his 'call up' papers from the German Komendatur telling him to report for work. He destroyed the letter and moved to work at Le Palais de la Bierre as a barman. German soldiers would visit and one told Raymond 'We're here to stay', 'Who says' said Raymond full of bravado, as the chef pulled him back into the kitchen away from trouble.

Like many other young men he wore the Cross of Lorraine (the emblem of the Free French, followers of Charles De Gaulle) in his lapel. It was noticed by a German soldier who stopped Raymond and poking a finger hard into his chest, gestured to the cross as he questioned him. Unable to understand German Raymond made the sign of the cross against his chest implying it was worn for religious reasons, and as the soldier sniffed and moved away he breathed a sigh of relief.

Within a few months he had been traced and an appointment to go for a medical reached him. He knew of people who had gone to attend a medical and not been seen again. Once again he moved on and started working as a labourer in a warehouse. Although he missed his cooking his priority was to earn money and stay alive so he kept on the move.

(See appendix for Raymond's own account of his wartime experiences.)

After the war he obtained a position as Commis Chef (2nd chef) at the 5 Star Hotel De L'Europe, one of the best hotels in Avignon. He was moving up the ladder with only one step more to Head Chef, he then worked for the Red Cross as a chef until May 1946 leaving them to work in Vichy.

After there he moved on to the Hotel La Mamounia in Marakesh, Morroco. Known as the 'white pearl' it was one of the best hotels in north Africa, visited by Winston Churchill, the King of Morocco, the King of Egypt and many other prestigious guests. He was to discover later that Lord and Lady Sefton also stayed there during this period. All the time Raymond was gaining valuable experience that was to take him to Croxteth.

Towards the end of the season the Head Chef would call his staff together and decide who was to stay on and who was to go to other hotels. Raymond was asked to return to Vichy to the Hotel Des Ambassadeurs, as a sous-chef until September 1947 when he was due to go to Algeria. A dockers strike stopped him and he worked as a Patissier preparing and creating desserts until 1948, the final piece in the jigsaw of his career.

While there, as a favour to a friend, he was asked to help out at a First Communion party as their caterer had let them down. These were always big family occasions with many friends invited and finished with a big evening meal for everyone. He joined the family for the day after being told there would be 'a lovely girl' there. He was to cook a full day's meals for the family and their many visitors. A seat was kept for him next to the only single lady there, 16 year old Elda, the girl he would marry.

It was during his last summer season at Vichy in the following year that he was offered the position that would change his life. 'How would you like to work in London?' he was asked. 'I don't speak English' he replied. 'You don't need to, it's very cosmopolitan' said his friend. 'Anyway it's at the French Embassy and I'll be at the Belgian Embassy'. It would be a new start for the friends, in England, where it was regular practise to employ a French chef and an English butler, the perfect combination.

At the end of the season the friends travelled to England. Arriving at Victoria they needed a taxi to take them to their new positions. Marching straight to a driver Raymond tried to give him instructions only to be tapped on the shoulder by a very big London Policeman. He pointed out the line of people waiting patiently for taxis. Raymond had never encountered the English custom of queuing. He had to learn quickly and returned to the back of the line. A short time later the two men and their luggage were collected by a diplomatic car, he could not resist smiling as they drove past the policeman still monitoring the waiting queue.

Once at the Embassy he soon discovered the chef had a drink problem. This had been overlooked by his employers until the day he was incapable of cooking and important guests were due. 'You'll have to take over' Raymond was told, 'I'm sure you can manage till we find someone else'. 'I can't' was his reply. 'What have you been doing these past weeks?' were his employer's final remarks as he left the kitchen, he knew what had been going on; Raymond was uncertain of how to carry on, a large dinner party was planned for the First Sea Lord. Help was at hand in the form of fellow chefs he met regularly. They came from the Belgian and Spanish Embassies and from the Savoy Hotel to help him. Each man took over a section of the preparation and cooking of the meal.

Although 'upstairs' knew he'd had help it was not mentioned when he was complimented 'Well done' on his achievements. He carried on working alone for almost two months until a new and permanent chef was found. This was to be Chef Gonin who had worked for the Duke and Duchess of Windsor in Paris. Raymond was to learn more in the months he worked under Gonin than he would have done during many years in France.

The many job changes meant he was always under the instruction of a 'new' chef. Their standard greeting was, 'Forget everything you have been told, you do things my way here'. This enabled Raymond to learn new dishes and different techniques in every position he held. It would all add to his store of knowledge and be used in his own kitchens at Croxteth.

Earl and Countess

Over the years Raymond and Elda built up a relationship with their employers. They respected the Earl and Countess who in turn valued the loyalty and service of the chef and his wife. They were allowed to order whatever was needed then sent the invoices to the office for payment. Raymond never had to explain himself or account for his spending at the Hall. He learned to 'read' his mistress and always knew the best time to 'request' a favour or make a change at either residence, he usually got his way.

One Christmas he received a cigarette lighter costing £5 as a present. Almost a week's wages. His special position meant he was the only member of staff allowed to own a car. Purchased in 1955 it had a left hand drive for the intended return to France. Another time they wanted to spend their holiday seeing parts of England. With the permission of the Countess they loaded their car with provisions from the Hall and drove to a deserted Abbeystead. Here they slept in their usual room and looked after themselves while visiting nearby Blackpool and the Lake District.

Earl & Countess of Sefton

The Countess was very fond of dogs and would often have her Yorkshire terrier following her looking for titbits from the kitchen. Raymond was not pleased to have the animals in his domain but unable to ban his employer's pets. He found them better than the distractions of many other houses - children, nannies and a governess. On visiting the kitchen the small dog lifted his leg and relieved himself against the table. Raymond was annoyed but could not say. He twisted a teatowel and flicked it at the dog without his mistress seeing. The lesson was learned, the dog kept his distance and behaved himself from then on.

The dogs were fed on rabbits killed on the estate. They would be skinned and cleaned before arriving at his kitchen for cooking then a valet would add dog biscuits and serve his small charges.

Lord Sefton liked his dogs to be exercised every day and if unable to do it himself would delegate the task to a footman or valet. Sometimes the footman left them in the Brush Room while attending to his duties. One day Lord Sefton returned early to discover this, his disapproval could be heard around the Hall as he punctuated the unfortunate man's telling off with his stick hitting the floor.

A regular habit of the Countess was to send handwritten notes down to the kitchen thanking Chef for his work. The short message sometimes written in pencil, 'Monsieur wants me to thank you for the delicious lunch' signed Josephine Sefton, always gave Raymond pleasure and spurred him to create new dishes for his employers.

On a rare night out in Liverpool Raymond and Elda went to one of their favourite haunts, the Gaumont cinema, only to find themselves a little way behind the Countess and her friend who were being shown upstairs by the manager. As the Countess reached the top she looked round, seeing them she called out 'Hello Chef, Madame' and turning to Lady Derby said, 'This is my chef and his wife' causing them a lot of embarassment.

If they went out to see friends they often got chatting late into the night and on their return would push their car through the large gates so as not to disturb anyone. After only a couple of hours sleep they would be back on duty making breakfast. If the Earl knew of his chef's outing he never said anything. As long as meals were served on time he was happy. He made a point of always checking with staff that his chef had returned from any outing or trip away from Croxteth with a simple 'Have they returned?'

Lady Sefton was less formal than her husband. She had been brought up in America where traditions of service and class were not as ingrained as in England. Although she adopted the English way of life and concerned herself with a number of Liverpool Charities she kept her American spontaneity often coming to chat with Elda. Their conversations were held in French so as not to be overheard knowing she would never betray her confidence.

When Elda was recovering from an operation she came down to their quarters behind the kitchen to visit. 'How is Madame?' she asked a surprised Raymond. 'In the sitting room, my Lady' he replied. 'May I see her'. Not waiting for a reply the Countess moved through the kitchen towards their living quarters. Raymond hurried ahead to warn his wife but the Countess swept in to the room before him. Noticing the changes that had been made since her last visit before Raymond's arrival and marriage, she looked around stating 'You are comfortable in here' Then sitting down she slipped off her shoes and curled her legs up on the chair to chat.

Each morning the menu for the day would go to the Countess on her breakfast tray. She would then choose from a list submitted by Raymond and let them know how many to cater for. She would accept it or cross out something she did not want, the returned card always carried a lingering whiff of her perfume, Chanel No 5. When visiting the kitchen later, around noon, Raymond would inform her it was 'too late to change'. The Countess would accept his word as she had no knowledge of cooking letting it slip one day that she thought omelettes were prepared in advance. Returning from one of her trips to France she started to tell Raymond of a meal she had enjoyed - Duck in wine sauce with black cherries. He could not help saying "You are not telling me how to cook duck are you My Lady?' She just smiled but was gracious enough to comment when he served it a week later, 'Perfect Chef!'

After one dinner party the coffee was being prepared to go upstairs. It was always served in one of the family's silver coffee pots. This was put down on the still warm, Aga. A lop sided pot was discovered by the chef as the silver started to melt, sending small silver pellets rolling about the cooker. Another one was quickly found and served but Raymond was very worried. He took the damaged pot to show to the Butler, 'Oh my God - what happened?' he asked turning pale. Raymond took the blame and full of apologies asked if it could be restored. The pot was sent away and on its return Raymond asked how much it had cost. 'You don't want to know' said the Butler and never mentioned it again. Many years later, after the death of the Earl, he watched as the pot was sold at auction for £5000.

Lord Sefton enjoyed most food but was not a lover of pork, 'Had too much of it during my time in India' he would say. He preferred ham, this often stretched Raymond's skills as he tried to inject variety into his menus. Lady Sefton was always careful not to choose anything the Earl might not like. When she was away Raymond tried different things, the Earl often coming down to say 'That was lovely Chef' which made all Raymond's efforts worthwhile and allowed him to serve it on another day.

Raymond with Blue Ford Zephyr

One day lunch was ordered early as the Countess was going into Liverpool to visit her dentist. Unfortunately the chauffeur was out with Lord Sefton but she knew chef was going shopping. 'Will you take me into Liverpool?' she asked. Raymond could hardly refuse. Driving his Ford Blue Zephyr 4 around to the front door of the Hall his mistress got into the front seat beside him. A very nervous chef drove the 6 miles into Liverpool breathing a sigh of relief on reaching her dentist. The next day after sorting the menus she said 'You drove well yesterday chef' and smiled. Raymond had no wish to repeat the exercise, he had never driven so carefully in his life!

The Seftons had Christmas Lunch at Croxteth Hall on alternate years. They were great friends with Lord and Lady Derby, their next door neighbour in stately home terms. He'd come to them with other guests for lunch on Christmas Day and they would visit him on Boxing Day. The following year they would switch around. This meant the staff (who were required to wait on) would have their Christmas on the day the Seftons went to Knowsley Hall (home of the Earl of Derby). Even on these special days Raymond and Elda ate alone but joined in with staff celebrations for weddings and birthdays. When the son of one member of staff married he made them a superb wedding cake.

Sometimes they were joined by the local 'bobby' making his 10.00 pm call. The police patrolled regularly as part of their duties but it was also a good place for a cup of tea and a chat. While they were there trays would often return to the kitchens unfinished from the upstairs dinner party. These 'leftovers' were a much better meal for the officers than the police canteen.

Fire

One Saturday in the summer of 1952 Chef and Elda had been out for the afternoon on a bike ride. 'Upstairs' were out and not expected back until later when they were to be joined by Lord and Lady Derby for dinner. Going into their quarters they could smell wood burning, this was unusual but thought it was in the grounds. Raymond went to check his kitchen and could see smoke outside. He walked past their lounge window, where Elda was watching then suddenly ran back again shouting 'The Hall's on fire' pointing to the flames trying to escape through the windows. He ran to find the Butler then continued on upstairs with a fire extinguisher. Opening the door of one room he was beaten back by the flames. Rooms panelled with wood over a hundred years old burned quickly and fiercely. 'Get out, Get out' he shouted as the alarmed Housekeeper appeared from another doorway.

As they hurried out he could hear the Butler's calm measured tones on the phone to the Clerk of Works 'You'd better come down, the Hall's on fire' They rang the servants bell to raise the alarm and tried to save what they could. Elda had opened the windows of their ground floor quarters and was throwing out everything she could onto the lawns. Fire appliances came from all over the area, from Birkenhead across the River Mersey and from Warrington.

Hoses rained water from the ponds onto the Hall in an attempt to stop the fire spreading but one wing was severely damaged along with its contents. Along with other staff Raymond helped to rescue carpets, valuables, anything they could carry. As they tried to get a large painting down a flight of stairs, they slipped in the rush to get it outside and it caught on the bannister/bend in the stairs ripping the portrait. He was later called to Lady Sefton to explain how the damage had happened. Every item damaged or otherwise had to be accounted for with the Insurance Company. The family's priceless collection of Sevre china was housed in display cabinets along the principal corridor of the Hall. No-one could find the key so they broke the glass to rescue as many pieces as they could carry.

By nine o'clock that night the fire was under control and the damage was being assessed. Lord Derby and the Agent arrived to see Raymond in the kitchen. 'What will we do tonight?' asked the agent. Raymond was amazed 'What can I do?' he said looking around him. His kitchen was under water, the walls, cupboards and work surfaces were blackened with smoke. 'Do not worry' said Lord Derby, 'Everyone will come to Knowsley' (his stately home on land adjoining Croxteth). Lord and Lady Sefton and all their staff, many of whom were very upset, went for the night. Not only had their place of work been burnt so had their living quarters and all their belongings. The shocked maids had only the clothes they stood up in.

Croxteth Hall on fire

Raymond and Elda did not go. Their flat was habitable and a valet also stayed. Waking next morning Elda saw a hand come through their ground floor bedroom window and pull back the curtain. She came face to face with a policeman, 'I'm sorry' he said on seeing her shocked face, 'I thought the place was empty' Elda was more shocked when she found out the ceiling above them was holding 4 inches of water which could have come through at any time during the night.

Getting up they started the job of cleaning the kitchen. It was covered with mud and running water was feeding through from the upstairs rooms. Raymond needed to get his kitchen functioning again ready for the return of staff and gentry later in the day, they would still expect meals to be served on time. Outside, the Hall was a sorry sight. The fire had burnt through to the roof, charred and burnt beams stuck out into empty spaces, with charcoal remnants of furniture balancing precariously. 'Why did you not come to Knowsley?' the Countess asked later 'Everything would have been left open' he explained, 'the food in the larders, the hall was not secure' The Earl and Countess did not forget his gesture.

The fire had been accidentally started by a workman employed to repaint the Library. A blowtorch had been used to remove the old varnish. When he went home for the day leaving it hot a spark was thought to have got behind the wooden panelling and smouldered, the heat caused tins of paint to explode shattering the windows and fanning the flames. One wing of the house was lost to the fire, starting on the first floor and burning through to the roof taking with it priceless items of furniture and possessions belonging to the Earl and his staff. The Earl moved across the corridor into another wing of the house. After repairs had been made to the roof and the rest of the building made safe the burnt out wing was closed off never to be restored or used again.

After the fire the Earl became a regular visitor to the kitchen. He would often stride in after being out riding and would sit on the corner of a table his long legs spreading across the floor as he asked in halting French 'How are you today Chef?'

The Christmas following the fire was another the Seftons decided to spend in America. This gave Raymond and Elda a rare opportunity to spend a long visit with their family. A replacement cook was to arrive at Croxteth from London at the beginning of December. They would leave straight away to spend Elda's birthday in France followed by Christmas and New Year. The cook failed to arrive and as Lady Sefton informed them their trip would have to be delayed until after Christmas, Elda could not stop the tears and quickly left the kitchen. The Countess tried to ease her distress with a cream leather travelling case for her birthday. The opportunity to use it came on Boxing Day as they left for France. Their families delaying the Christmas celebrations until they arrived from England not returning until February in time for the Hare Coursing.

She was just as caring when family came from France to visit her chef. On hearing they were looking for somewhere to stay she instructed 'See the Butler'. Raymond's family were then given the use of rooms normally used by visiting servants at no charge. As the Earl and Countess were away Raymond was able to show them around the Hall. His visitors were amazed at the richness of their surroundings. He was equally proud to show his family how well he had done in his new life.

When the Earl died after a short illness in 1972, his funeral was an emotional affair leading the Countess to say 'I never expected to see grown men shedding tears like this'. She was moved to see how much affection the staff had for the Earl. Although she continued to live at Croxteth for a while Lady Sefton then moved between London and Abbeystead. According to the Earl's wishes the Hall and parkland were given to the people of Liverpool and the contents sold at an auction held in the grounds by Christies.

A huge marquee was erected for the sale which attracted many local people. A huge white cross marked the landing for helicopters bringing other interested parties and dealers from all over the world.

Although Lady Sefton asked Raymond and Elda to go to London with her, first to the London house then to a smaller property at Eaton Square, they declined knowing how cramped the accommodation was. They opted to remain at Croxteth moving into their first home, a converted mews flat over the 17th century stables in the grounds outside the Hall, provided for them and other staff under the terms of the Earl's will.

Later on in the mid 1970s she again hinted in a letter they would be welcome to join her household at Abbeystead.   She was having a new flat prepared for the chef, but by then Raymond was building up his own business after being told his references showed he was 'overqualified' for any local establishment.

Elda outside their converted mews flat

The Countess took a great interest in this, often writing to them on her portable typewriter to see how business was. She would also ask 'her chef' to prepare some of her favourites like chicken or salmon mousse. These would be collected by her chauffeur and taken sometimes to Abbeystead. Raymond's business, 'Le Petit Gourmet', was based in Aintree and many of his buffets were delivered to the racecourse previously visited by so many of Croxteth's guests. One day a gleaming Daimler drew up outside his shop front, the local shoppers watched in awe as the chauffeur got out of his seat and walked round to open the car for its occupant. Out stepped the Countess and went into the shop. After her visit his neighbouring shopkeepers couldn't fail to be impressed by his visitor. She was to write later 'I loved your little shop'.

Raymond went on to cater for the French Consulate and his guests. Then became a guest himself during a visit by the French Fleet, before retiring due to ill health. His longest period of service had been for the Earl. The visits to 'his' kitchen now see Heritage Guides in the costume of Victorian maids relating the Hall's history. Raymond has no need to join the groups of interested visitors. He has lived and worked through some of the events surrounding the noble family and declares 'It was a privilege to work for Lord Sefton. Hard work but so rewarding and worthwhile. A different world with the kind of life we will never see again. I feel privileged to have been a part of it'.

Raymond and Elda's association with Croxteth Hall did not end with the death of Lord Sefton. They are valuable members of the Friends of Croxteth Hall and Country Park, a charity dedicated to support and promote the Hall.

Raymond & Elda

Appendix

My experiences between 1943 to 1945 during the German occupation of France.

by Raymond C. Lempereur

In 1943, I was 19 and working as a cook at the Hotel Terminus in Avignon. One day, I received a letter from the German Komendatur ordering me to present myself to become a member of the obligatory workforce; I decided not to go! I destroyed the letter, left my job at the hotel and took another as a barman at "Le Palais de la Bierre" in the rue de la Republique.

However, about two months later, I received another letter instructing me to go for a medical examination by German doctors. I knew, from the experiences of others, that if I went there I would not be allowed to leave the building so, once again, I decided not to attend.

On my way to work one day at the Hotel Terminus, I saw many cars and lorries there and a large number of German officers who had come to requisition it. They had already bisected the hotel's facilities - one side for themselves, the other for civilians. The kitchen had been divided, too, and two German cooks had been installed to cook for the Germans. They were very polite and we never had any problem with them.

One day, one of the Germans went out, leaving his hand-gun and holster hanging on a nail in the kitchen. Being curious, I moved to the other side of the cookers and took the gun from its holster; the metal was a dark blue. I was still holding it when I heard footsteps on the stairs - he was coming back! Quickly, I replaced the gun in its holster and hung it back on the nail, where it was still swinging gently when its owner returned. The German gave me a sidelong glance but said nothing; however, he never again left the pistol there when he left the kitchen.

Food was rationed severely but at the hotel we prepared the best food we could for our clients with the limited resources available to us. The Germans had plenty of meat but we had hardly anything. I remember that when my pal, Roger, and I went to work in the afternoons, the Germans used to leave large pans of sauerkraut, together with a lot of sausages and pieces of pork, cooking gently in their oven. As soon as the German cooks departed, Roger and I felt justified in helping ourselves to a plate of that or we would cut some roasting pork, eating it furtively in the kitchen whilst listening in case the others returned. They may have realised what we did but they never said anything to us.

Later, I found work at "Le Palais de la Foire", which was a warehouse used by French and German people to store furniture and provisions all the year round. I was merely a labourer there but at that time was prepared to do anything to have a wage and stay alive and I stayed there for two or three months. One morning, my work-mate, a young man named René, and I took a break from chopping wood and were having a snack in our little wooden hut when the door burst open and the German corporal (a beast of a man) came in shouting insults in German and signalling for us to return to work immediately. He had his hand on his pistol and I believed he was about to attack us so my reflex action was to defend myself and René, who was hiding behind me. I picked up my axe. The corporal stopped in his tracks and went out, to return half an hour later, flanked by two officers. They threatened us and withdrew.

I didn't wait to find out what their intentions were but left just before noon. Three days later, I was in Malaucene in the company of a group of other young men in a similar situation to mine. For a short while, I worked as a lumberjack until May 5th, 1944, when the pro-German Militia caught up with us.

At 6 a.m. on that day, my friend and I were on the working site, about to fell a tree, when we heard the sound of rifle shots, exploding grenades and machine gun fire. Looking down in the valley below us, we could see men from the Militia and mobile guards in Gestapo uniforms climbing towards us in the direction of the small hamlet of Suzette. Suddenly, they were upon us and we were surrounded by armed men pushing their weapons into our faces and backs and yelling at us not to move. They asked to see our papers, searched us and examined our hands. Looking at my still well-kept hands, they said, "You're no more a lumberjack than we are, young man!"

Looking at my identity card, their mood toughened. When the card had been rubber-stamped, part of the imprint had been on the photograph, part on the card itself but the ink had been rubbed off the picture with use - something I had never noticed. Believing that my ID was a forgery, they arrested me and my seven work-mates at once, putting handcuffs on us behind our backs. They marched all eight of us into Suzette, to a small farm where they beat up the old farmer cruelly, despite the pleas of his wife, until blood was running down his face.

In front of the farm there was a wall which I will never forget. Our captors made us face the wall with our hands upon it. With machine guns at our backs, we feared the worst but, after a while, they turned away and threw grenades at the farmhouse and burnt it down. It was as though they were playing some hideous game. Apparently, they had discovered some ammunition and mattresses (useful to the Resistance) at the farm.

While all this was going on, I recognised some Militia men from Avignon who were part of the expedition set up to seek out the 200 or so "maquisards" (members of the resistance) in the area. Of the two who appeared to be in charge, one was the owner of the "Hotel du Louvre", a man by the name of 'B', and the other was a boxer known as 'M' who had been misusing his skills to beat the young men.

Disappointed that there had been no maquisards at the farm, the Militia and the Germans took out their anger on us eight young men. They chose three of us and took them away in a van, returning an hour later without them. We never saw them again or found out what had happened to them. The rest of us were not tortured but were menaced and were told that if we lied to them we would be beaten, then sent to a concentration camp. Believe me, one never forgets moments like these!

We were put in lorries, two by two, bound in heavy chains but able to see out. On the road to Avignon, the convoy, with about 400 Militia, Civic Guards and Germans, stopped in the town of Vaison-La-Romaine. There, the enemy chased young people, firing guns and stealing provisions and anything portable they could lay their hands on. There was panic in the streets and we prisoners could see everything that was happening. Later, some lorries went towards Buis-les-Baronies.

*We arrived in Avignon at about 6 p.m. and were taken to the headquarters of the Militia in the Rue Joseph-Vernet which was notorious for the methods of interrogation practised there. However, the place was already over-crowded with prisoners so we went on to the Headquarters of the Police. They locked us up in cells, telling us, "Tomorrow, we will question you. The chief of the Militia and members of the Gestapo will be there and we will **make** you talk!" They pointed out another prisoner who had both his legs set in plaster and told us that he had been shot with a hunting gun whilst trying to escape; one of our guards said, "This is what will happen to **you** if you try to escape. Do you understand me?". We were given water but no food. You can imagine what sort of night we had, trying to sleep on concrete and anticipating the following day's ordeal.*

At 11 a.m. the next morning, they interrogated us one by one. When it was my turn, I was pushed roughly into a room where there were three grey-suited men seated at a table. On the table there were two hand-guns and a wooden truncheon. I was wearing only a sleeveless tee-shirt, trousers, shoes and socks; I was made to undress completely. They subjected me to an intimate examination to see if I was Jewish and went on to question me about my identity card which they believed was a forgery, asking who had made it and who had given it to me; they were aware that someone was supplying fake papers to people desperate to escape from the Germans.

I answered, truthfully, that my ID card was genuine. 'What', they asked, 'was a cook doing cutting down trees in the mountains?' and I answered that I knew nothing about what was happening in the Mont Ventoux, could not find a job in Avignon and so was working there to avoid being sent to Germany. They told me, " You will be deported to Germany!"

Next, I was taken to the school of Carmes (which is still in Avignon) and on the second floor there, was asked the same questions. The person in charge was an Inspector of Police - a tall man who was a known collaborator. (After the war, I learned that he was a Russian and had been shot by the Free French forces). That afternoon, we were taken to the Boulevard St. Ruff and were at last given some food. Our captors handcuffed us to a heavy chain and marched us through the town. Unwashed and unshaven, we looked more like convicted criminals in a chain gang, rather than innocent teenagers.

Our destination turned out to be the barracks of "La Caserne de Salle", notorious as the place where deportees were held. We were locked up on the second floor and were provided with straw mattresses which were full of fleas, lice and bugs. Another sleepless night began.

One week later, as we were standing waiting for medical assessment, I experienced a touch of human kindness which lifted my spirits. A lady dressed in white came to me and whispered, "Are you Raymond Lempereur and did you have polio as a child ?" I replied. "Yes. Why do you ask?" She went on to say, "Do what I tell you. When you start walking, limp. Exaggerate your polio symptoms because the German doctors are going to give you a thorough medical examination to see if you are fit enough for forced labour in Germany". Then my 'Angel in White' rejoined the group of doctors and I did what she suggested.

Unknown to me at the time, I had another helper; my Aunt Melanie Lempereur knew someone with high-ranking connections and learned of my arrest. Her contact was working alongside some German medicos and helped to persuade them to allow me to stay in France. Thanks to these two brave women, much later that afternoon I was given a pass which stated, "Required to work as a labourer on the railways". They kept my ID card and the contents of my wallet, including photographs and all the money I had - two months' wages.

So, I became a labourer at the railway yards where locomotives were repaired. The Germans had issued an order that all French citizens aged between 18 and 60 years should be made to guard French railway tracks. Groups for night shifts were formed. Operating in pairs, the men would patrol the rail-tracks, each pair covering a distance of about 250 metres. This was done to foil any attempt by the French Resistance to sabotage the railway lines. During the occupation, some young men - mainly teenagers - used to go out after curfew to try to immobilise the Germans' lorries. They did this by slashing tyres, damaging air valves and by putting sand or small gravel into their fuel tanks and water into the hydraulic systems. Shifts ran from 8.00 p.m. until 7.00 a.m. the following morning. We could not have cared less about protecting the railway lines, for if the Resistance had come - armed to the teeth - there would have been little that we could have done since we ourselves did not have any weapons.

Therefore, at night, especially in Winter, we would stay in our little hut, light a fire and cook a few potatoes or chestnuts over the embers; with our meagre snack and some wine which we had brought with us, we would spend some time pleasantly - carefree, cosy and warm! Luckily, we were never caught by the German patrols.

After two or three days working on the railway, about fifty of us witnessed a disturbing incident. About an hour after turning up for work one morning, we saw two black cars arrive with members of the Gestapo dressed, as usual. entirely in black. They stormed into the office and later emerged with the Director and his assistant whose faces were streaming with blood; evidently they had been beaten savagely.

It transpired that four or five locomotives had been sabotaged by the Resistance who had also damaged the locomotives' water pumps. The Managers were held responsible for this attack and were arrested. The cars sped away towards Avignon with these two men aboard. Because Avignon was an important rail centre, we were bombarded by the Americans. After six weeks of attacks, I had had enough and (in July, 1944) left. I found another labouring job in Chateau-Neuf, near Montelimar not knowing that the work entailed the construction of landing strips for German twin-engined fighter planes.

There were many young men like me working there, all with the same aim of avoiding deportation. We ate and slept in a large, barn-like house. After a week, the German police arrived and arrested our foreman on a charge of sabotage. We had been deliberately making weak mixes of cement, adding much more sand than cement. After the foreman's arrest, we were supervised more closely. About 11 o'clock one morning another wave of Allied 'planes flew over and bombed the place, destroying the airstrip and the adjacent aircraft sheds. After the raid, the Germans were edgy and were watching us intently; we were very nervous.

The next day, about fifteen of us were told that we were to leave the site and go to Avignon. We were loaded into a van, set off and saw a column of tanks heading north in retreat. The road we were on was littered with tanks, cars and lorries which had been destroyed in the raid and there were dead bodies everywhere. The horrors of war were all too evident. After driving for 60 kilometres or so, we were stopped by a Panzer division which was also in retreat. At gun point, they ordered us youngsters to come down from the lorry and checked our ID's and passes. I was particularly apprehensive because my pass was one signed only by the German police.

The Germans seemed indecisive about what to do with us until one of their officers arrived, had a discussion with them and, much to our relief, allowed us to move on to Avignon. And there I stayed until the liberation when, about 20th August, 1944, the Americans, Allied troops and Free French forces arrived in the South of France. The war was over. I had survived!

In 1945, I was told that 'B', the acting chief of the pro-German Militia at the time I was arrested, was in prison. I was chief witness at his trial - indeed, I was the only witness left of those arrested at Mont-Ventoux, the others having been deported, never to be seen again. 'B's wife, who owned a hotel, called for me and offered a pile of money, which she had on the table before her, as a bribe to buy my silence. I refused. I was given police protection for quite a while until the trial because I received death threats. In 1946, 'B' was sentenced to life imprisonment and I was glad that my friends had been avenged; he died later of cancer.

After having had a successful career as a chef in England for 24 years, first at the French Embassy in London and subsequently as chef to the Earl of Sefton, my dear wife, Elda, and I decided to make what we considered to be a pilgrimage back to the scenes of my war-time experiences. So, in the year 2000, we returned to Malaucene and again met with people who remembered all that had happened.

Among them was an 85-year old lady who, over a glass of Muscatel, recounted all the events with amazing detail. She recalled that the Militia were angry that members of the Resistance had fled the day before the air-raid and had deployed 400 or so troops in lorries to seek them out. The people of the village were demented with fear that reprisals would be taken against them because everyone there had been supportive of the Resistance in many ways including supplying food and allowing them to move from farm to farm. The local villagers also helped young men like me - perhaps regarding us as potential recruits for Resistance. Certainly I would have joined if they had asked me.

My wife and I also visited the farmhouse at Suzette which had been burned down. It had been rebuilt and the present occupiers gave us coffee and I made my way to 'my wall', where I had almost met my death. Again, I faced it and placed my hands upon it, as I had been forced to do so many years before. It was a very emotional experience. I re-lived my efforts to avoid deportation, helped by my family and friends.

So many people suffered during the occupation. In my own family, the uncle of my half-sister, who held extreme left political convictions, was sent to the infamous Buchenwaldt concentration camp; my cousin, Louis Coste, was deported to a German working camp in 1942; my elder brother, Andre-Louis, who was in the airforce, perished when the ship he was on, 'L'Armoriciere', sank as he was coming home on leave. In Avignon Town Hall, there is a plaque which commemorates Andre-Louis as one of the war heroes who died fighting for France.

Now aged 77, my memories of those eventful years, 1943, 44 and 45, are as vivid today as ever and it is only recently that I have felt able to speak openly about them. Now, this is my true account.

RAYMOND C. LEMPEREUR,
August 23rd, 2002.

With Thanks to David Dunn for his help